MISSION ACCOMPLISHED

MISSION
ACCOMPLISHED

WICKED CARTOONS BY AMERICA'S
MOST WANTED POLITICAL CARTOONIST

KHALIL BENDIB
FOREWORD BY NORMAN SOLOMON

Interlink Books

An imprint of Interlink Publishing Group, Inc.
Northampton, Massachusetts

Dedicated to the memory of Karl Linn

Many thanks to Barbara Lubin, Inno Nagara, Pratap Chaterjee, Peter Phillips, Brian Johns, Jack Foley and my agent, Sara Powell.

First published in 2007 by

INTERLINK BOOKS
An imprint of Interlink Publishing Group, Inc.
46 Crosby Street, Northampton, Massachusetts 01060
www.interlinkbooks.com

Library-of-Congress Cataloging-in-Publication Data
Bendib, Khalil.
Mission accomplished : wicked cartoons by America's most wanted political cartoonist / by Khalil Bendib.
    p. cm.
ISBN 978-1-56656-691-9 (pbk.)
1. United States—Politics and government—2001—Caricatures and cartoons. 2. Bush, George W. (George Walker), 1946–
Caricatures and cartoons. 3. Political culture—United States—Caricatures and cartoons. 4. American wit and humor, Pictorial. I. Title.
E902.B458 2007
320.97302'07--dc22
                            2007006182

Printed and bound in China

To receive a copy of our 40-page color catalog, please call 800-238-LINK, write to us at the above address, or visit our website at
www.interlinkbooks.com

CONTENTS

FOREWORD

In this time of satellite-guided missiles and computer-generated graphics, a political cartoonist can go to work with nothing more than a pen. The best outcomes run directly counter to the artificial fog and lethal hypocrisy that dominate the media landscape. Many cartoonists go through the motions, but few are able to fulfill the potential. This book accomplishes the mission—in direct opposition to the policy-makers and elites who thrive on war and inequities.

Open this book at random, and you'll see a couple of cartoons that tell you much more about the real world than the latest edition of the *New York Times* can manage. Khalil Bendib will never snuggle into (as he puts it) "an embedded media ... putting America to sleep." In the best traditions of political art, his creations offer vantage points with lines-of-sight that contradict the favorite angles of mass media.

Mission Accomplished is about point of view. The cartoons invert the U.S. media "reality"—which is to say, the cartoons subvert media unreality—by focusing on disputes and debates in human terms. For the typical American viewer, listener, and reader, this book's P.O.V. is a world turned upside down. The modern-day princes and potentates, the wealthy investors and powerful politicians, are stripped of their pretensions and placed in context of their effects on vast numbers of individual human beings.

From ground level, Khalil Bendib helps us to see—and, in the process, cuts through hazy illusions. An unspoken precept of news coverage often elevates the humanity of people in one group over another. The media juxtapositions routinely encourage us to choose between two sides—fundamentalist zealots in Washington or Tehran, wanton killers on one side or another in Iraq, competing teams of religious fanatics who are eager to slaughter in the name of their particular faith.

This book refuses to accept such false choices. Bendib's cartoons scramble a deck that has been stacked by the demagogues and crusaders who feel that they must diminish the humanity of others to exalt their own. Along the way, the cartoons in *Mission Accomplished* may strike some American viewers as harsh—and no wonder, since the baseline of political cartooning in the United States is so unwilling to step hard on the hooves of such sacred bovines as Israel, the "Defense" Department, and the 21st-century version of American corporate capitalism.

"The most sacred cow of the press is the press itself," the great media critic George Seldes commented many decades ago. And today, despite surface potshots, the mainstream news outlets are by and large notably respectful of their own prerogatives and corporatized sensibilities. In such a media environment, the need for the pen-and-ink work of Khalil Bendib is greater than ever.

No wonder he can lay claim to being "America's most censored political cartoonist." This guy keeps breaking the unwritten rules that keep daily newspaper cartoonists within well-understood boundaries. When the day comes that the lives of Palestinian children and Jewish children are treated with equal reverence by U.S. news media, Khalil Bendib might consider taking a well-earned long sabbatical. But in the meantime, his sharp pen is badly needed.

Likewise, when news coverage reflects the fact that (in the words of GOP-airbrushed Adam Smith) "labor creates all wealth" instead of the other way around, the need for Bendib's cartoons on economic justice will not be so great. And when equitable health care or environmental protection becomes more important than maximizing the profits of major investors, this book might not even need a sequel.

But in the world you and I live in, we need all the help we can get! So keep on drawing, Khalil Bendib!

—Norman Solomon, author of *War Made Easy: How Presidents and Pundits Keep Spinning Us to Death*

1

NEW ORLEANS:

MAKE LEVEE, NOT WAR

4

5

6

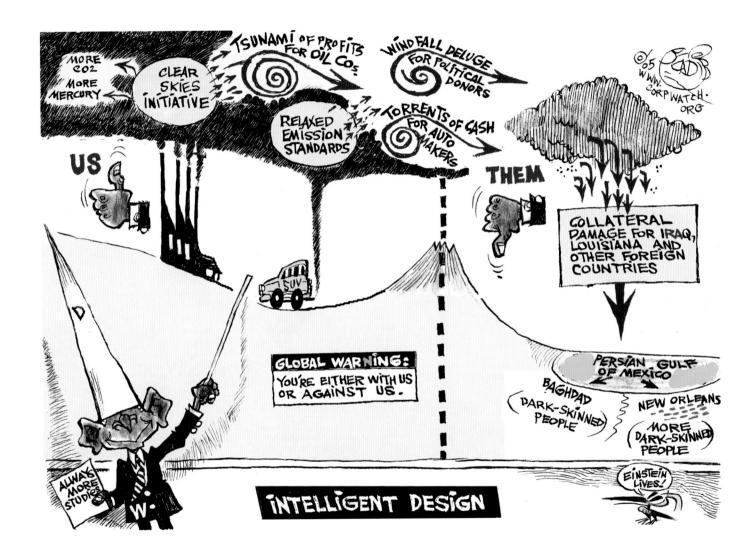

WAR PROFITEERING:
AIN'T NO BID LIKE NO-BID

13

16

EMPIRE:
BETWEEN IRAQ AND A HARD PLACE

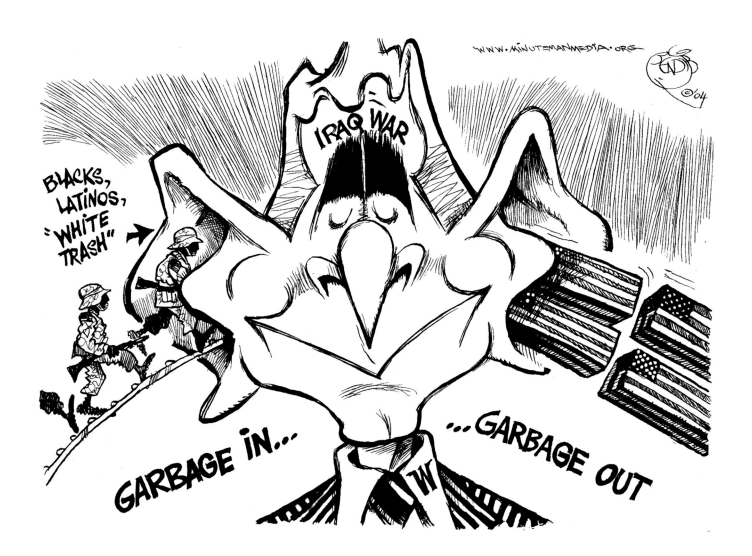

WWW.MINUTEMANMEDIA.ORG

IRAQ WAR

BLACKS, LATINOS, "WHITE TRASH"

GARBAGE IN...

...GARBAGE OUT

W

©'04

19

21

23

THE DEFINITION OF INSANITY: TO KEEP DOING THE SAME THING AND EXPECT DIFFERENT RESULTS.

26

27

A Fair and Balanced MEDIA

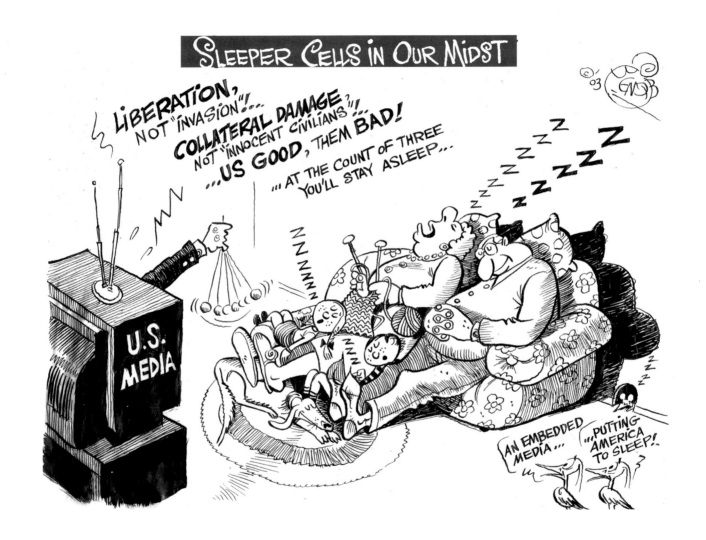

33

36

37

39

PALESTEIN: THE WALL

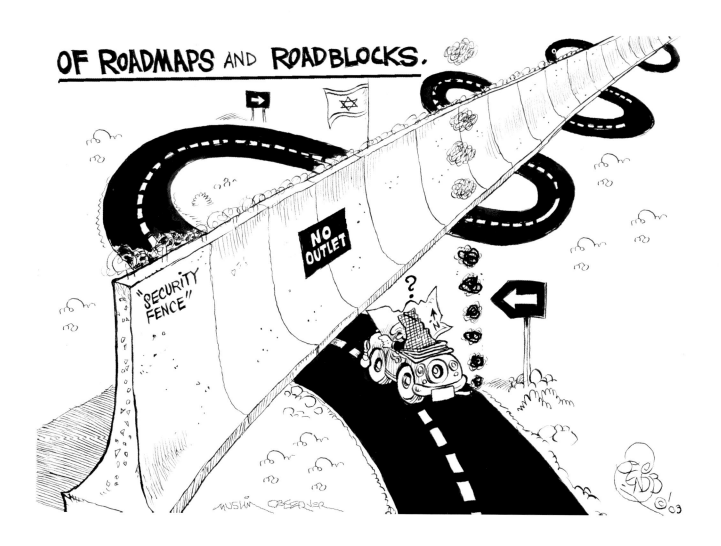

49

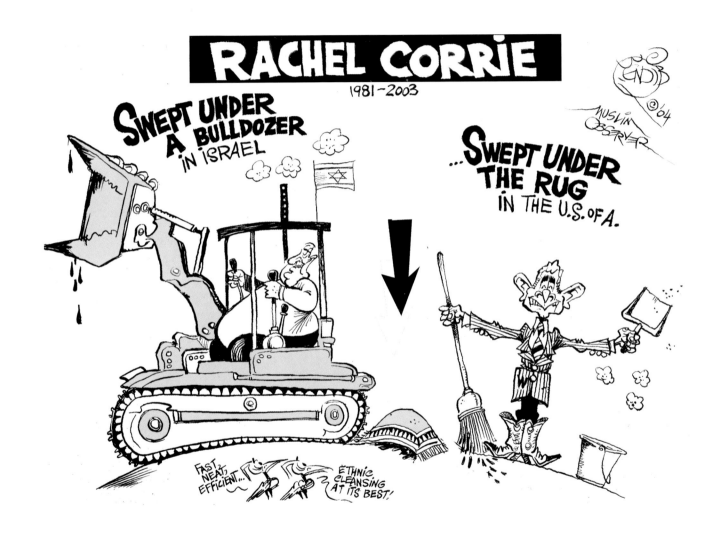

51

52

53

54

55

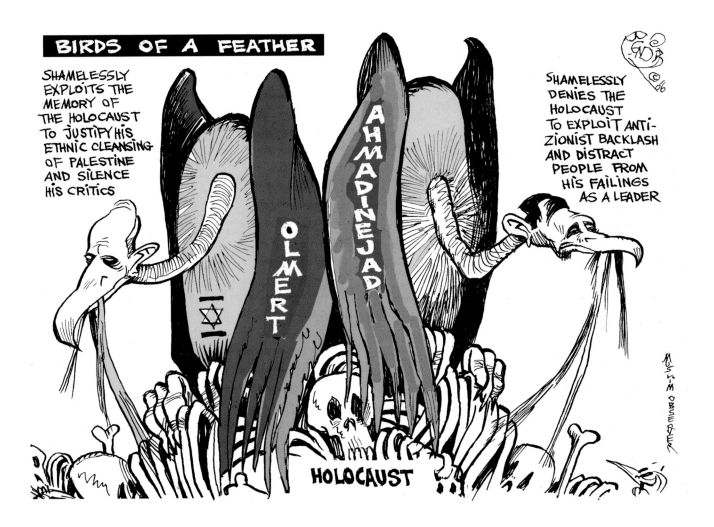

BIRDS OF A FEATHER

SHAMELESSLY EXPLOITS THE MEMORY OF THE HOLOCAUST TO JUSTIFY HIS ETHNIC CLEANSING OF PALESTINE AND SILENCE HIS CRITICS

OLMERT

AHMADINEJAD

SHAMELESSLY DENIES THE HOLOCAUST TO EXPLOIT ANTI-ZIONIST BACKLASH AND DISTRACT PEOPLE FROM HIS FAILINGS AS A LEADER

HOLOCAUST

MUSLIM OBSERVER

BREATHING WHILE BLACK

60

I'LL KEEP OUT THE **EXTERNAL** ENEMY WHILE YOU KEEP OUT THE **INTERNAL** ENEMY...

65

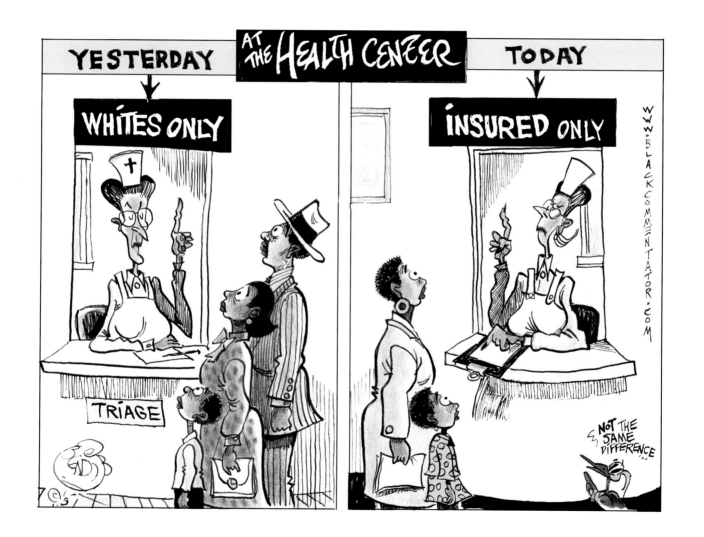

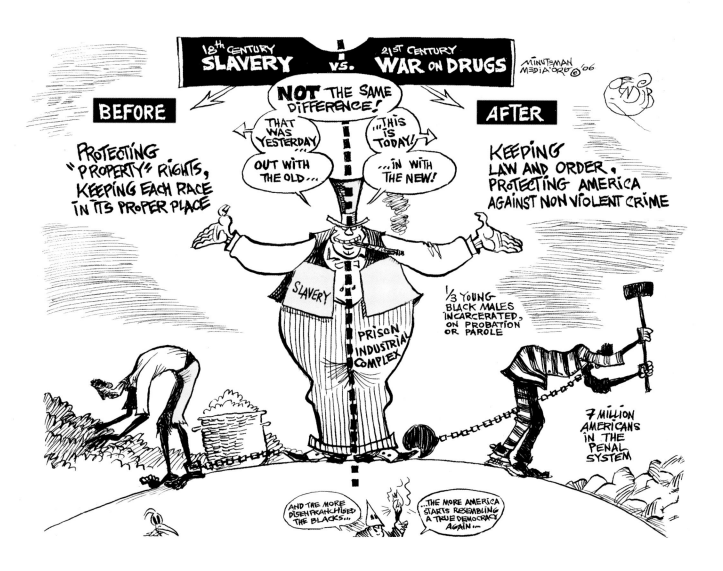

73

DEMOCRACY BEGINS AT HOME

I used to HATE Americans because of their freedoms, but all I feel any more is a mixture of fondness and admiration....

87

89

BIG DEAL! I'VE BEEN GIVING THE FINGER TO THE WHOLE COUNTRY AND THE WORLD FOR MORE THAN FOUR YEARS AND IT'S NEVER HURT MY BUSINESS

ISLAMOPHOBIA:
(HOLD THE DANISH)

93

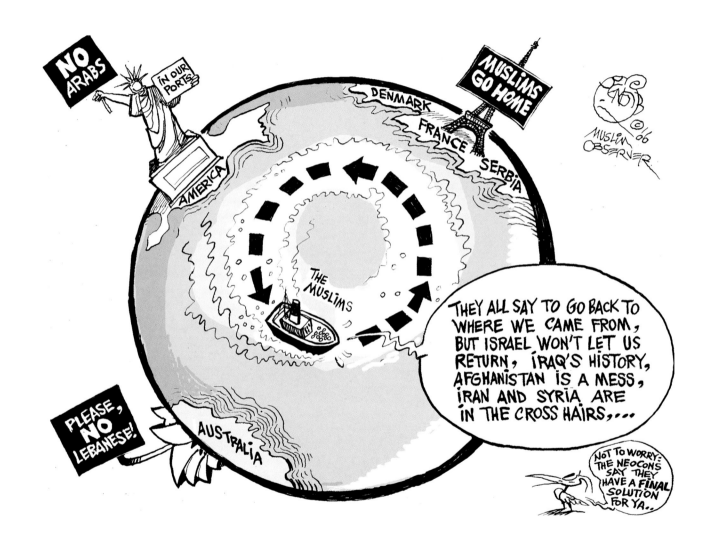

100

REVENGE OF THE CRIMINALLY INSANE

SO FAR, I'VE FOUND THE REMAINS OF TWO KORANS, ONE BILL OF RIGHTS, A GENEVA
CONVENTION, A HABEAS CORPUS.....YOU GUYS EVER HEARD OF TOILET PAPER?

NUKES-R-US
(NOT THEM!)

SEARCHING FOR LICE OF MASS DESTRUCTION IN ALL THE WRONG PLACES

MIRROR, MIRROR ON THE WALL, WHO'S THE MOST STRIDENT OF THEM 'ALL?
MUSLIM OBSERVER
© '06
MISSION ACCOMPLISHED
FISSION ACCOMPLISHED
W
IRAN
SEPARATED AT BIRTH?

111

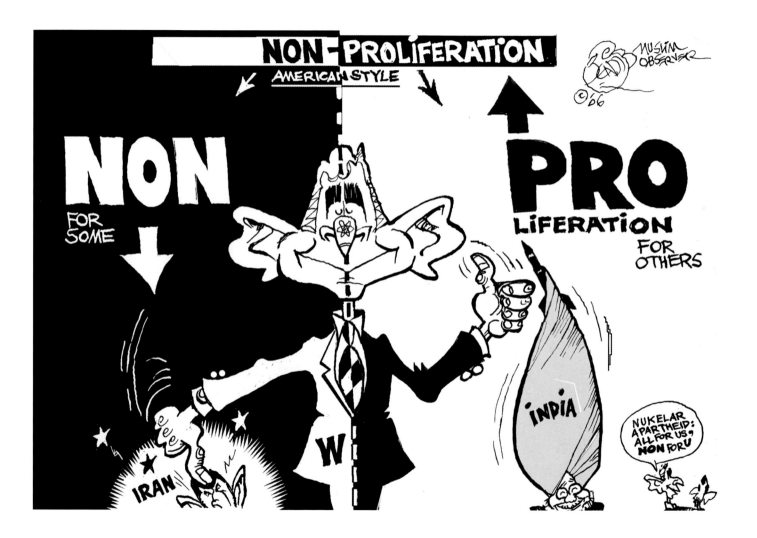

LABOR PAINS

115

1492: LOOKING FOR INDIA, CHRISTOPHER COLUMBUS DISCOVERS AMERICA INSTEAD, AND DECIDES TO PRETEND THAT AMERICANS ARE REALLY "INDIANS!"

AWESOME TANDOORI, YOU GUYS! BURP!

C.C.

AMERICA

2004: LOOKING FOR EVER CHEAPER WHITE-COLLAR LABOR, CORPORATE AMERICA DISCOVERS INDIA AND ASKS INDIANS TO PRETEND THEY'RE "AMERICANS"

CUSTOMER SERWICE. THIS IS WICTOR. VHAT CAN I HELP YOU VITH?

WATCH THOSE Vs AND Ws RAJ...

©04

WWW. CORP? WATCH. ORG

CEO

INDIA

WHO'S U.S. PRESIDENT? G.V. BUSH OF COURSE, VHY?

124

FOOD FOR THOUGHT

133

134

SACRED COW

Planet Earth:

Global Warming or Nuclear Winter?

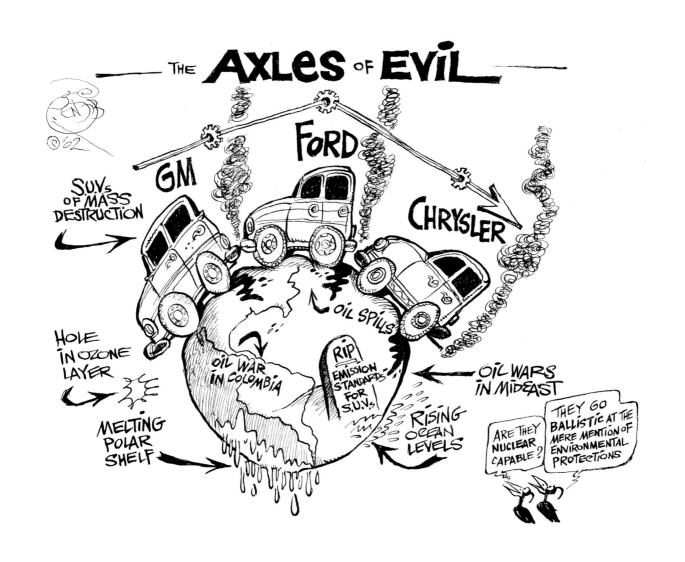

141

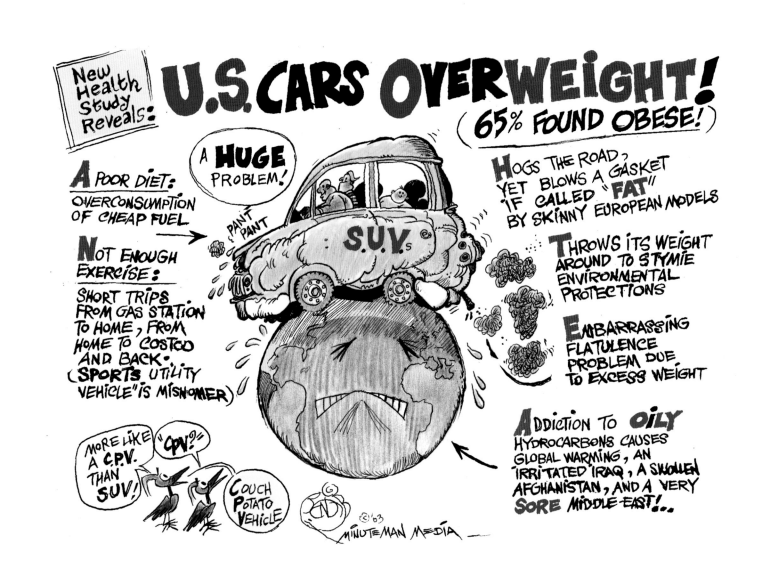

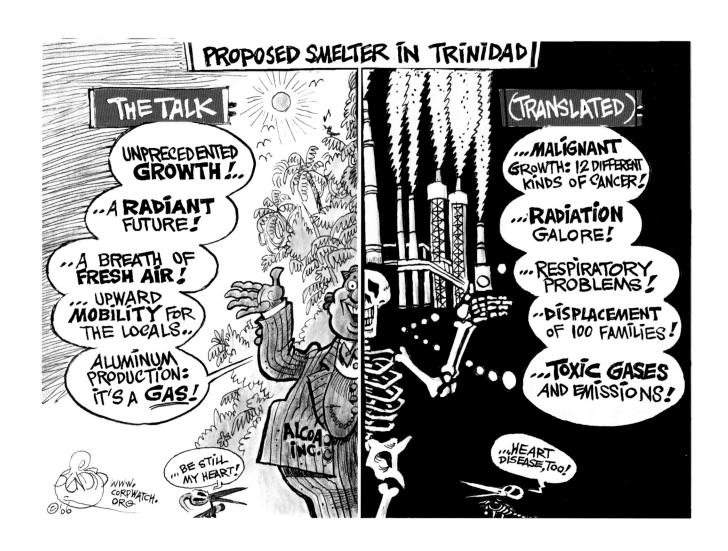

149

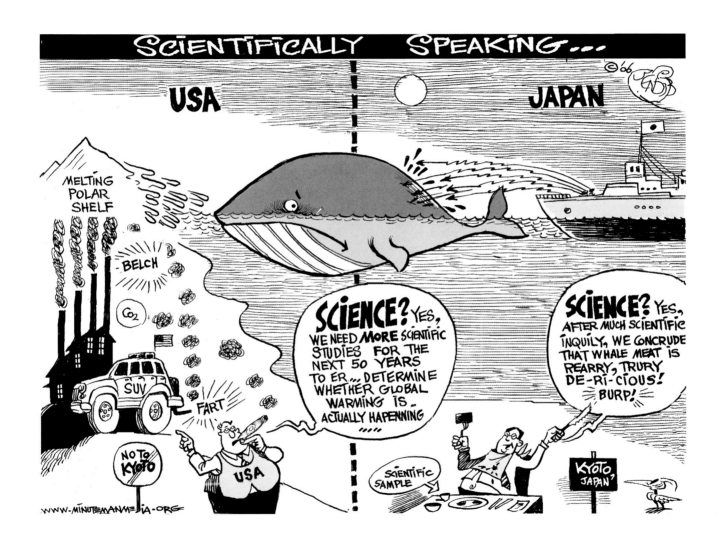

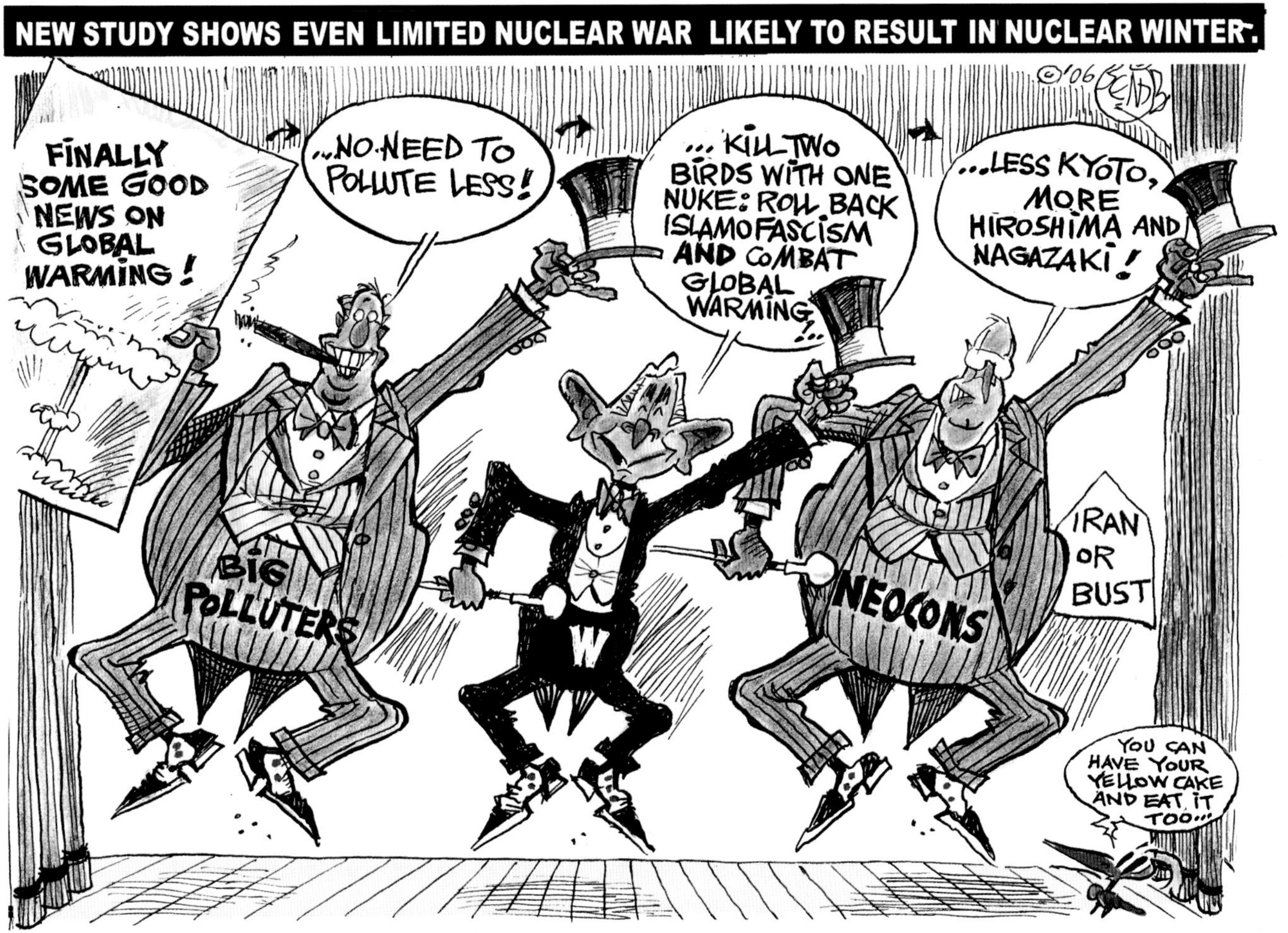
NEW STUDY SHOWS EVEN LIMITED NUCLEAR WAR LIKELY TO RESULT IN NUCLEAR WINTER.
FINALLY SOME GOOD NEWS ON GLOBAL WARMING!
...NO NEED TO POLLUTE LESS!
... KILL TWO BIRDS WITH ONE NUKE: ROLL BACK ISLAMOFASCISM AND COMBAT GLOBAL WARMING...
...LESS KYOTO, MORE HIROSHIMA AND NAGAZAKI!
BIG POLLUTERS
W
NEOCONS
IRAN OR BUST
YOU CAN HAVE YOUR YELLOW CAKE AND EAT IT TOO...

SINNERS AMONG US

155

156

157

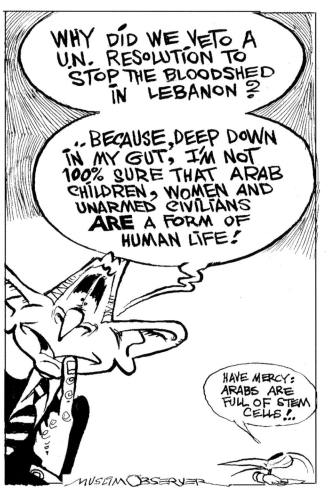

A GENDER AGENDA

DAMNED IF YOU DO, DAMNED IF YOU DON'T...

165

167

EDUCATION:
"Is Our Children Learning?"

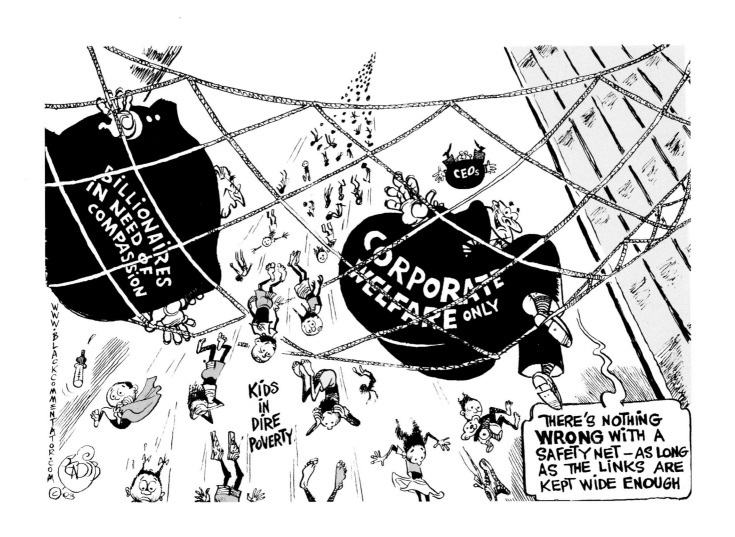

MOTHER AFRICA

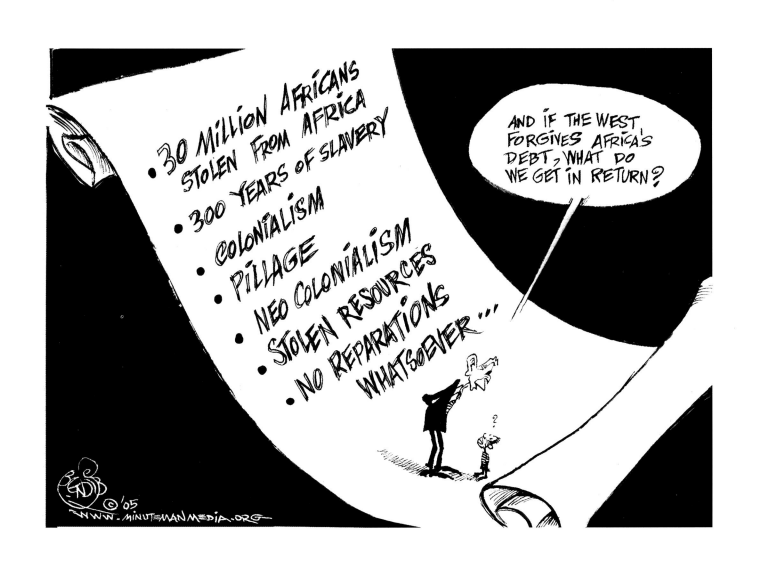

181

183

THE GOLDEN YEARS

187

189

About Khalil Bendib

A survivor of the infamous Battle of Algiers, award-winning Berkeley-based political cartoonist Khalil Bendib voted with his feet at age 20 by coming to America to seek refuge from the political censorship he experienced in his native land at an early age upon the publication of his first cartoons—only to find comparable challenges in the Land of the Free.

In a post-9/11 world where Muslims, Arabs and other people of color are fast becoming the proverbial canary in the mineshaft of American democracy, Mr. Bendib's powerful and hysterical cartoons sound a salutary alarm, interjecting a unique and much needed, non-Eurocentric perspective into a largely homogenized American political discourse.

Khalil Bendib revels in puncturing inane platitudes and hackneyed stereotypes that pass for factual information in our increasingly conservative mainstream media, never hesitating to question some of our most cherished assumptions. Wherever other established cartoonists and journalists see a sacred cow and reverently steer clear, Bendib recognizes opportunities for shish-kebab and sharpens his pen in gleeful anticipation.

Mr. Bendib's cartoons are distributed by Minuteman Media News Service to over 1,700 small and mid-size newspapers across North America and are regularly featured in many small magazines and web sites worldwide. They have also appeared in the *New York Times*, the *Los Angeles Times*, *USA Today* and numerous other large American newspapers. More of his work can be seen at www.bendib.com

"Khalil Bendib always delights me with his intellectual and extremely poignant, often times sadly funny, cartoons. This book should be required reading for all concerned with social justice everywhere!"

—Cynthia McKinney

"These cartoons are brilliant and stunningly humane. Khalil Bendib is one of the best (if not the best) political cartoonists drawing today."

—Gray Brechin

"With his scathing and brilliant humor, Mr. Bendib connects the dots of the American political landscape like no other cartoonist alive today."

—Michael Welles Propper

"With epic ferocity and compassion, Khalil Bendib's cartoons have the uncanny ability to translate for us what reality looks like to people stuck on the other side of the rail road tracks — that is, 90% of the world's population."

—Song Ngo Chin